All God's Creatures

Photographed and hand painted by Kathleen Francour
Stories by Sylvia Seymour

Photography: © 1997 Kathleen Francour
Carefree, Arizona. All rights reserved.

Copyright © 1997 Publications International, Ltd.
All rights reserved. This publication may not be reproduced or quoted in whole or in part by any means whatsoever without written permission from Louis Weber, C.E.O.

Permission is never granted for commercial purposes.
Jesus Loves the Little Children is a trademark of Publications International, Ltd.
Manufactured in U.S.A.

ISBN: 0-7853-2122-5

PUBLICATIONS INTERNATIONAL, LTD.
7373 North Cicero Avenue
Lincolnwood, Illinois 60646

A Home for Boomer

Malcom saw a dog. "Where did you come from?" Malcom stooped to pet the dog. "Are you lost? You can come live with me. I'll name you Boomer."

"Mommy, Mommy! Look what I found! May I keep Boomer, Mommy, please?!"

Mother reached down and scratched Boomer's ears. She noticed the collar and tag. "Malcom, I know you really want Boomer, but he already has a home. We'd better take him back to his own family."

"He has a family?"

"Yes, and they are probably worried about him. Jesus would want the dog to be with his own family."

"You found Jasper!" said the owners. "Oh, thank you! We've missed him so much."

"You know, Mom, I think Jesus is glad we took Boomer back to his home. Bringing Boomer home was the right thing to do."

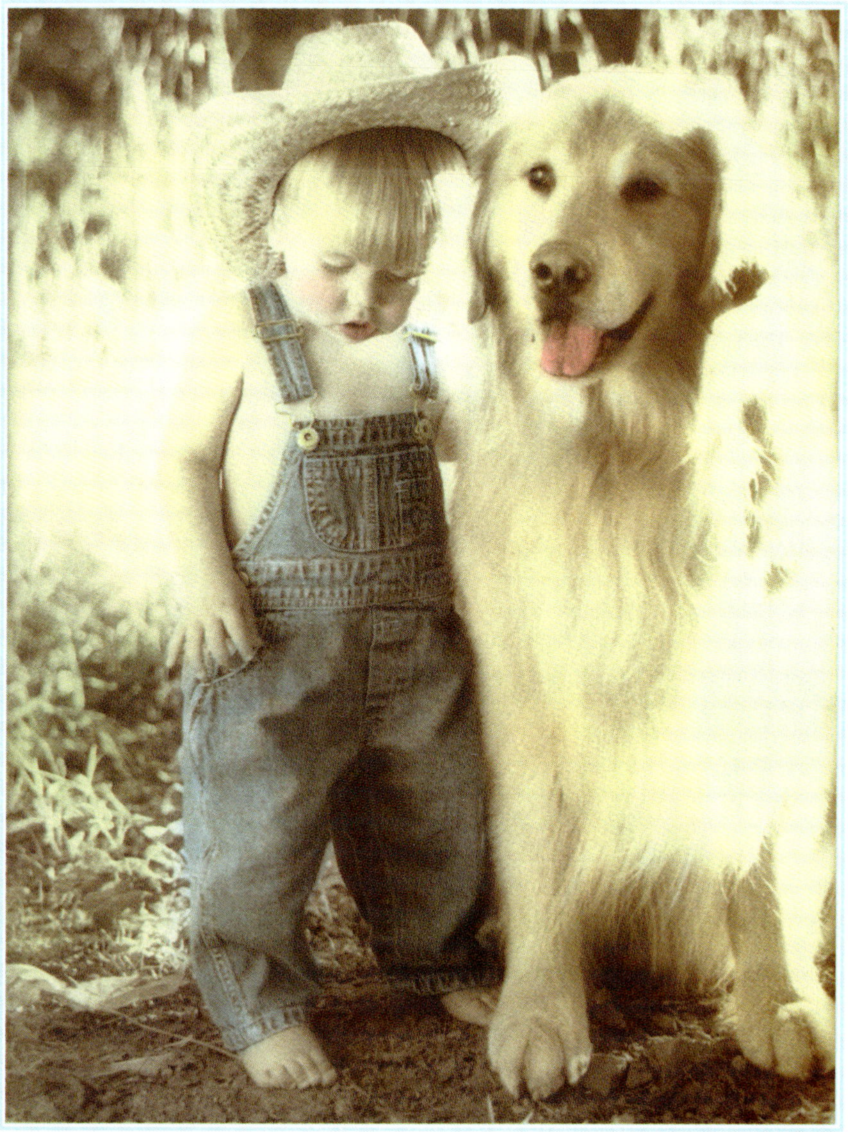

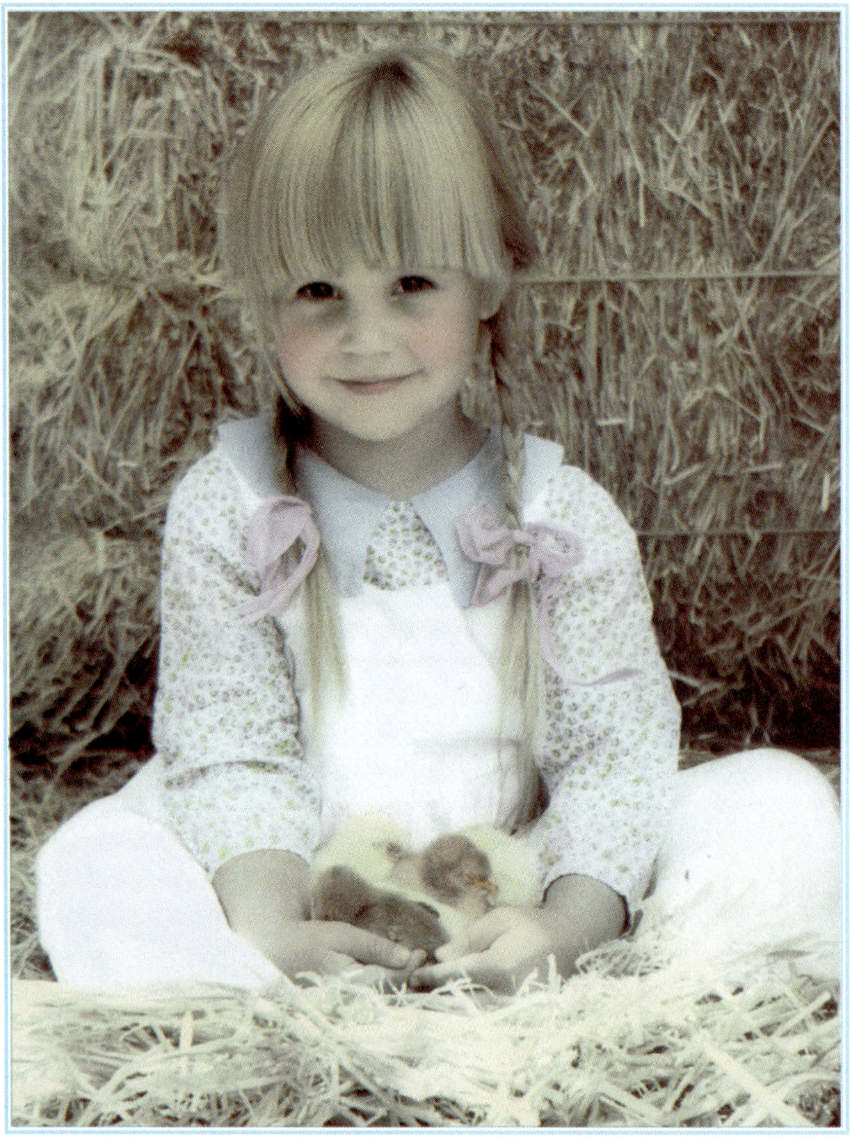

You are to me, O Lord,
 what wings are to the flying bird.

Dear Father, hear and bless
 Thy beasts and singing birds.
And guard with tenderness
 Small things that have no words.

Hear my prayer, Lord Jesus,
for our friends the animals.
Give to them all Thy mercy and pity,
and all compassion from those who
deal with them.
Make all hands that touch them gentle,
and all voices that speak to them kind.
Help us to be true friends to animals,
so that we may share the blessings
of Thy mercy.
For the sake of tender-hearted Jesus Christ
our Lord.

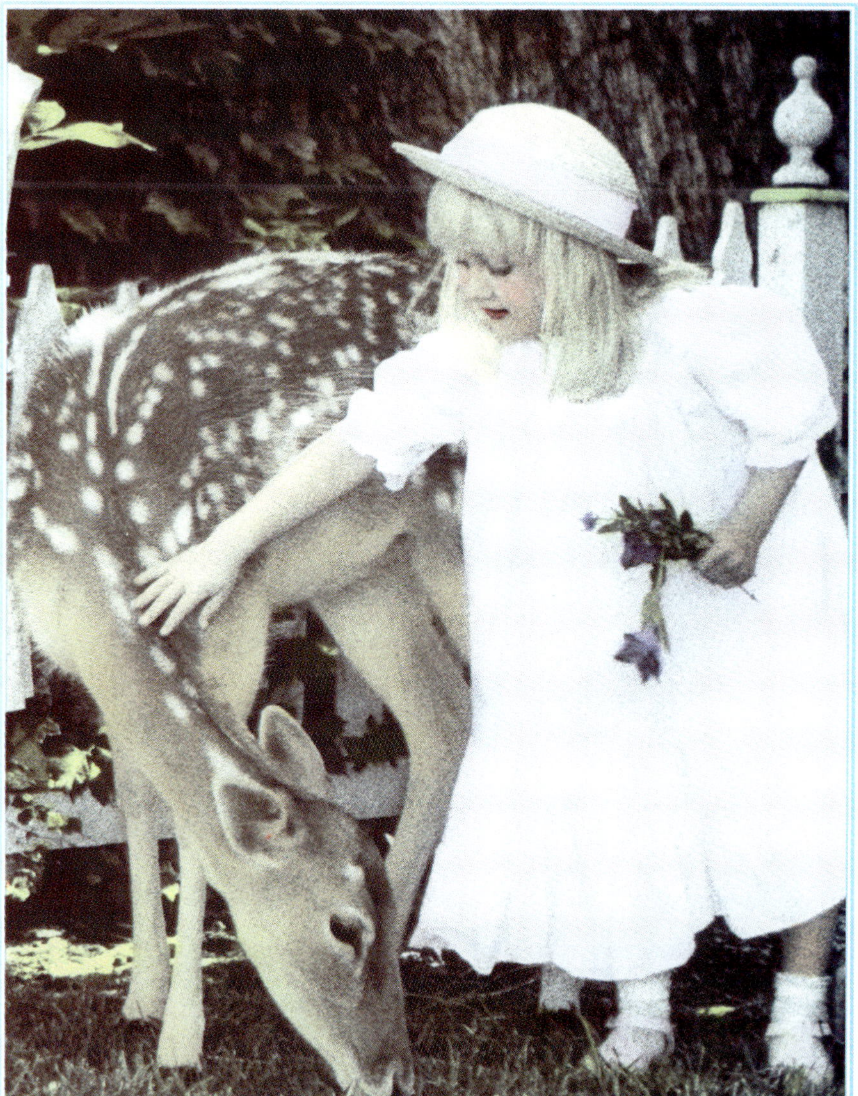

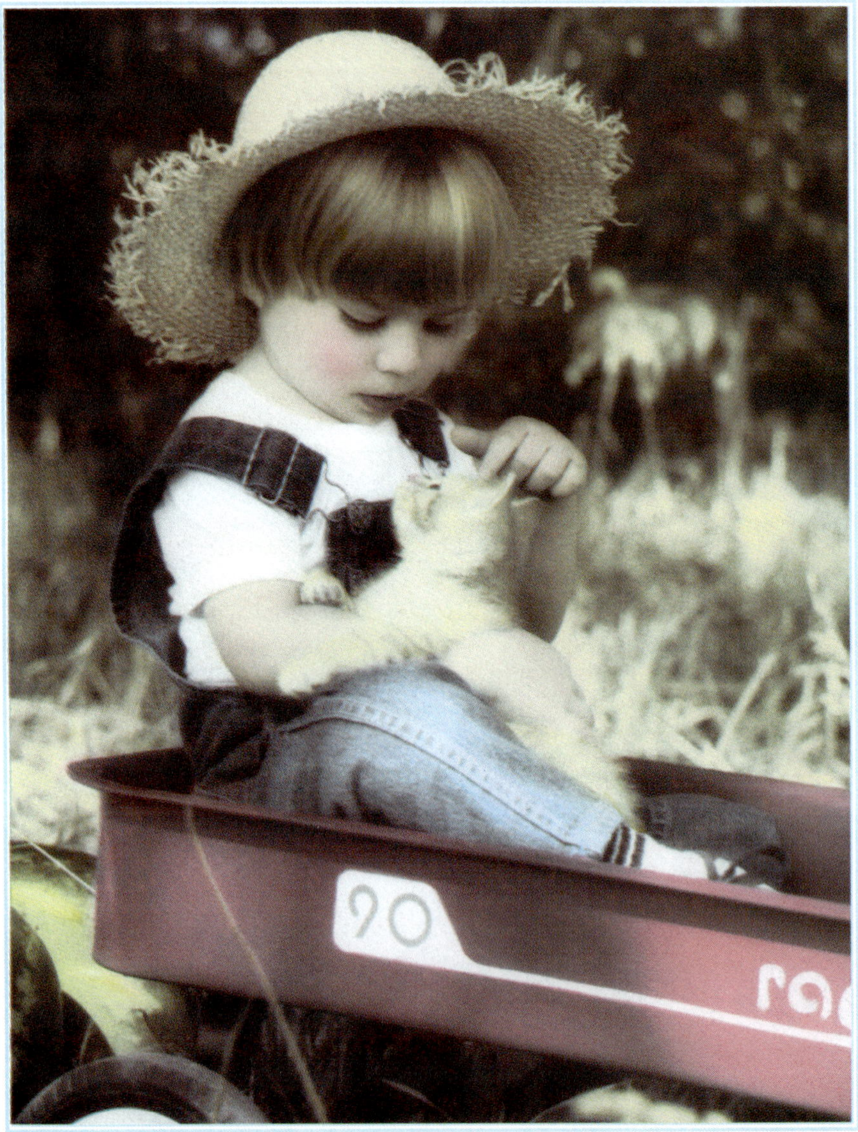
90

The Hungry Kitten

"Martin, have you fed your kitten?" asked Mother.

"I forgot."

"Remember, you promised to take care of your kitten if we let you keep her."

"I'll do it tomorrow. I want to play now."

"Meow," said the hungry kitten.

Martin looked at the tiny kitten. She looked so helpless. She didn't have a mommy to take care of her. "God made this kitten and God made me," Martin said to himself. "Jesus would want me to care for her just like He cares for me!"

"Meow."

"I think Jesus wants me to feed my kitten right now. Mommy, where's the cat food?"

If a rabbit had words,
it would thank You for its ears.
If an elephant had words,
it would thank You for its trunk.
If a zebra had words,
it would thank You for its stripes.
If a cat had words,
it would thank You for its whiskers.
But since only I have words, dear Jesus,
I will thank You for them all!

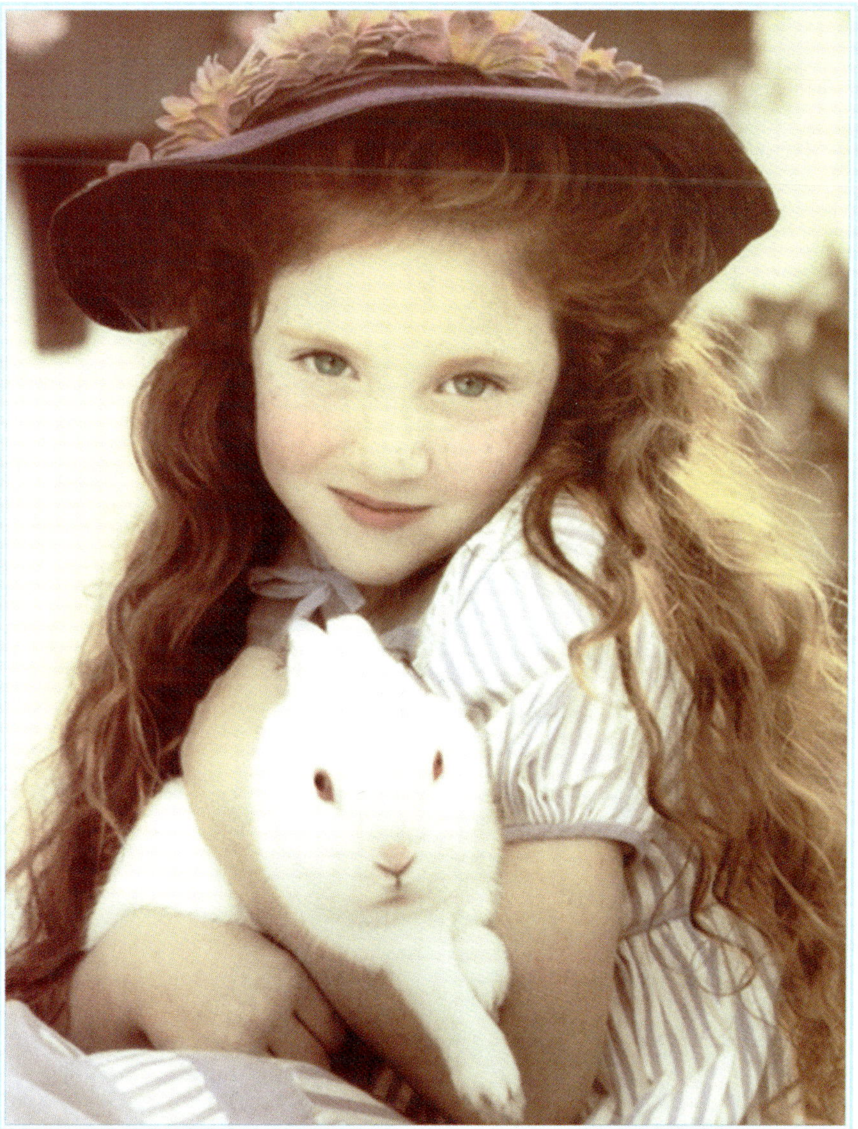

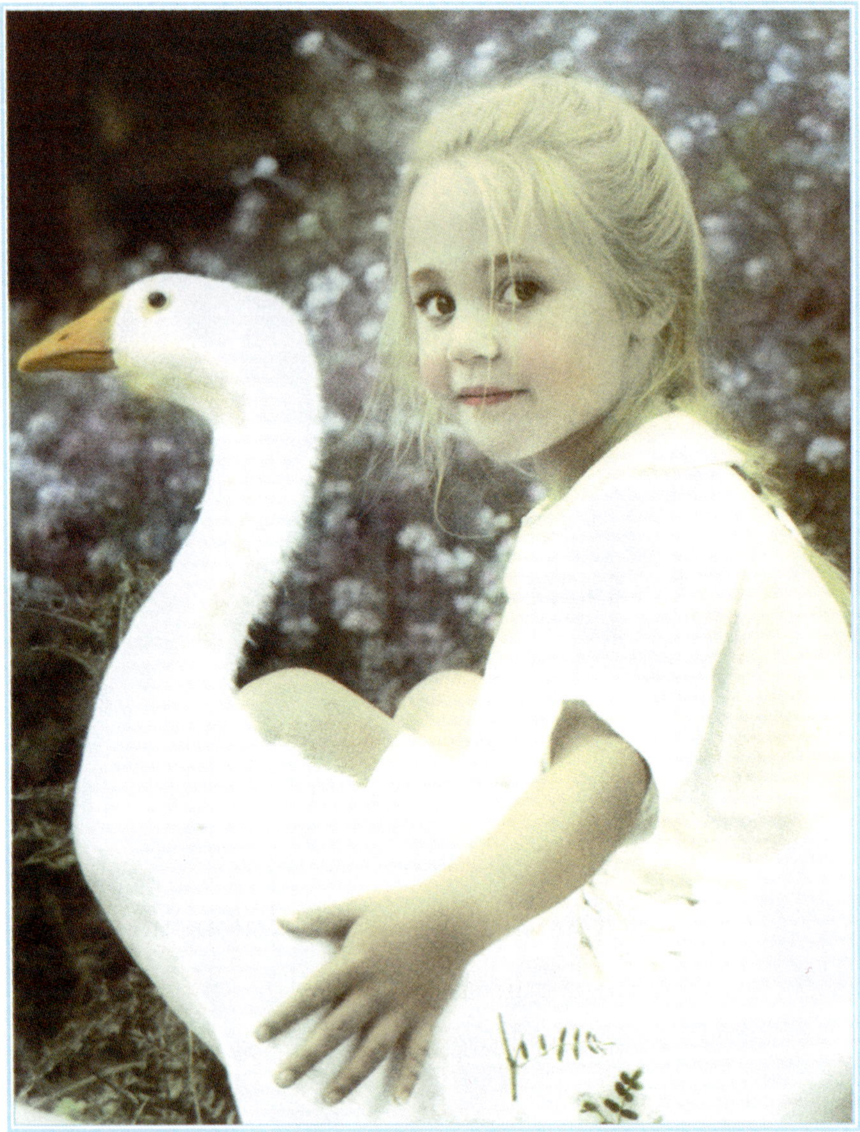

All things bright and beautiful,
  All creatures great and small,
All things wise and wonderful,
  The Lord God made them all.

Cecil Frances Alexander

The birds above me;
the kitten on my lap;
the toad that hops;
the deer that runs;
Lord Jesus, it was You who
created all these wonderful animals.
Thank you, Lord.
They are treasured.

A Visit to the Zoo

"I love the zoo!" Margaret chattered happily as she skipped from one place to another. She noticed how different the animals were. "Look at the big hippo. Look at the tall giraffe with the long, skinny neck!"

Grandmother smiled as Margaret observed the animals. "The zebra has stripes. The leopard has spots. I love the elephant's long nose."

Margaret paused and looked at her grandmother. "Did God make ALL the animals?"

"Yes, God made them all."

"Does God love the animals the same way even when they're different?"

"Yes," Grandmother smiled. "And He loves all the children in the world, even when they're different."

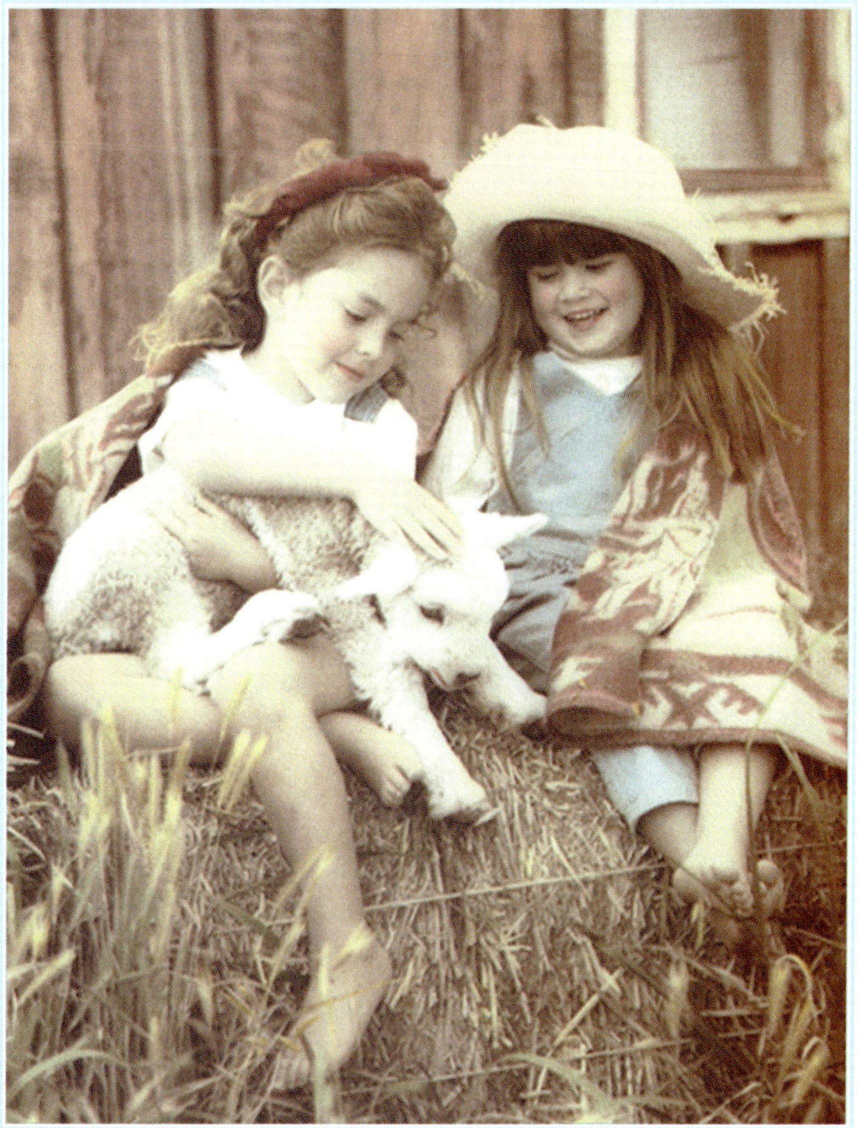

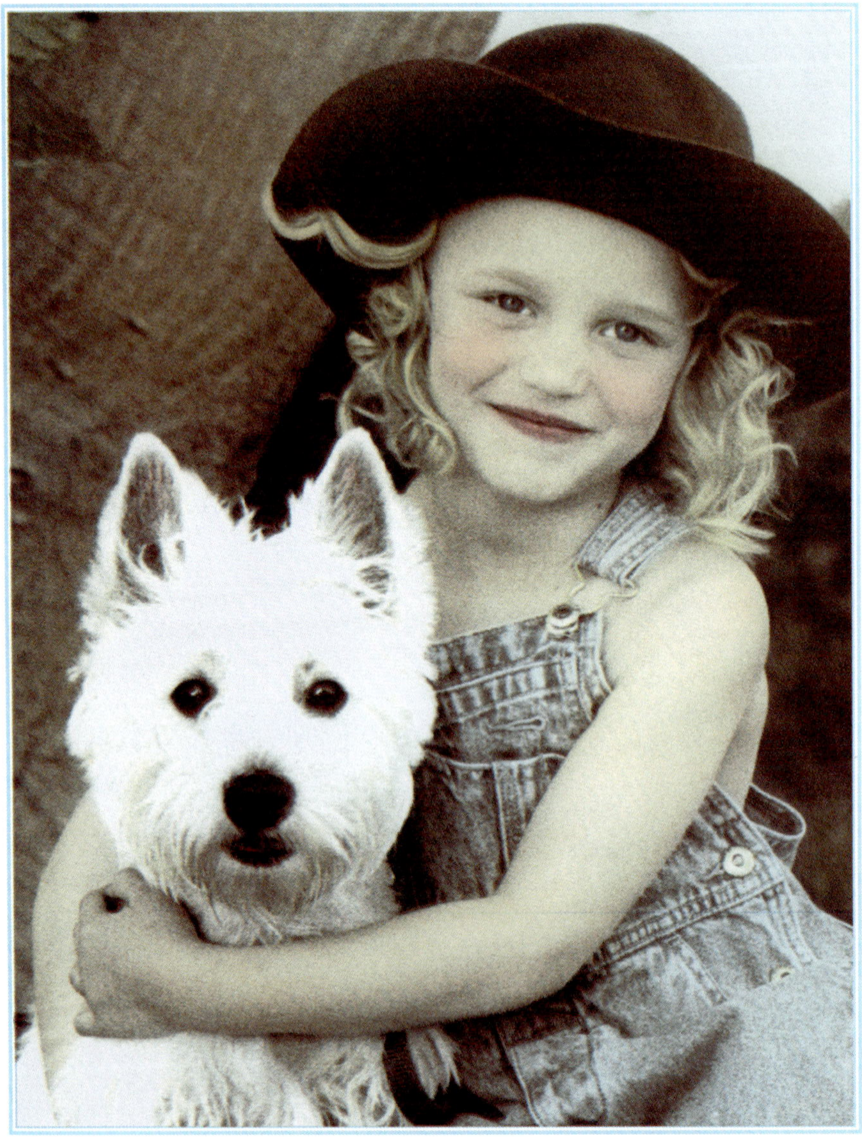

Lord Jesus,
Bless my tiny puppy
as he sits at home all day.
For he is so brave and believes himself
to be a great watch dog, while still so small.

Dear Jesus,
Sometimes all I need to do is
look at my dog watching me,
and I know I am being taken care of,
in more ways than one.

Something so tiny as a butterfly
can hold all the love of Jesus.

Praise God, from whom all blessings flow!
 Praise Him, all creatures here below!
Praise Him above, ye heavenly Host!
 Praise Father, Son, and Holy Ghost.

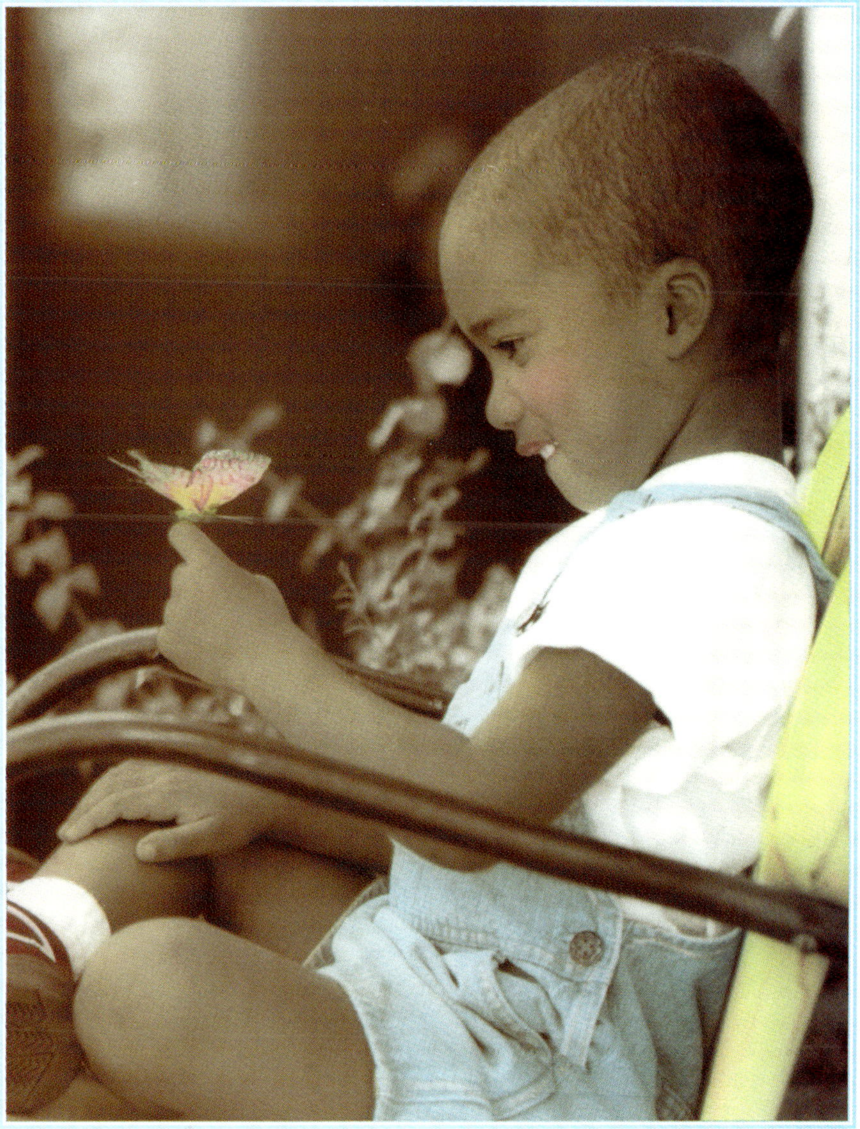

He prayeth best, who loveth best
    All things both great and small;
For the dear God who loveth us,
    He made and loveth all.